The NFL's Greatest Teams

Denver Broncos

Big Buddy Books
An Imprint of Abdo Publishing
www.abdopublishing.com

Marcia Zappa

www.abdopublishing.com

Published by Abdo Publishing, a division of ABDO, PO Box 398166, Minneapolis, Minnesota 55439.
Copyright © 2015 by Abdo Consulting Group, Inc. International copyrights reserved in all countries. No part
of this book may be reproduced in any form without written permission from the publisher. Big Buddy Books™
is a trademark and logo of Abdo Publishing.

Printed in the United States of America, North Mankato, Minnesota.
092014
012015

Cover Photo: ASSOCIATED PRESS.
Interior Photos: ASSOCIATED PRESS.

Coordinating Series Editor: Rochelle Baltzer
Contributing Editors: Bridget O'Brien, Sarah Tieck
Graphic Design: Michelle Labatt

Library of Congress Cataloging-in-Publication Data

Zappa, Marcia, 1985-
  Denver Broncos / Marcia Zappa.
    pages cm. -- (The NFL's Greatest Teams)
  Audience: Age: 7-11.
  ISBN 978-1-62403-585-2
  1. Denver Broncos (Football team)--History--Juvenile literature. I. Title.
  GV956.D37Z37 2015
  796.332'640978883--dc23
                        2014026418

Contents

A Winning Team

The Denver Broncos are a football team from Denver, Colorado. They have played in the National Football League (NFL) for more than 40 years.

The Broncos have had good seasons and bad. But time and again, they've proven themselves. Let's see what makes the Broncos one of the NFL's greatest teams.

Orange and navy are the team's colors.

League Play

Team Standings

The AFC and the National Football Conference (NFC) make up the NFL. Each conference has a north, south, east, and west division.

The NFL got its start in 1920. Its teams have changed over the years. Today, there are 32 teams. They make up two conferences and eight divisions.

The Broncos play in the West Division of the American Football Conference (AFC). This division also includes the Kansas City Chiefs, the Oakland Raiders, and the San Diego Chargers.

The Raiders are a major rival of the Broncos. Fans get excited when they face off!

Kicking Off

The Broncos started out in 1960. They were founded by businessman Bob Howsam.

The Broncos were one of the first teams in the American Football League (AFL). In 1970, this league joined the NFL.

Like many new teams, the Broncos struggled early on. They didn't have a winning season until 1973.

Early Broncos stars included powerful running back Floyd Little (*center, dark jersey*).

Bob's Bears

Bob Howsam owned a minor league baseball team called the Denver Bears. The Broncos played in Bears Stadium. Later, it became known as Mile High Stadium.

Highlight Reel

Win or Go Home

NFL teams play 16 regular season games each year. The teams with the best records are part of the play-off games. Play-off winners move on to the conference championships. Then, conference winners face off in the Super Bowl!

After 1973, the Broncos started having winning seasons regularly. In 1977, the team made it to the play-offs for the first time. They went on to their first Super Bowl in 1978. But, they lost to the Dallas Cowboys 27–10.

In 1983, star quarterback John Elway joined the Broncos. He helped the team get back to the Super Bowl in 1987, 1988, and 1990. But, they continued to lose the big game.

The Broncos lost the 1990 Super Bowl 55–10 to the San Francisco 49ers. This was the worst loss in Super Bowl history.

Elway is famous for a comeback known as "the Drive." He led the Broncos 98 yards to a touchdown. It tied the score in a 1987 play-off game.

In 1995, Mike Shanahan took over as head coach. He led the team back to the Super Bowl in 1998. This time, they won! The Broncos beat the Green Bay Packers 31–24. They won the 1999 Super Bowl, too! They beat the Atlanta Falcons 34–19.

In 2011, Elway rejoined the Broncos as a businessman. He helped the team get star quarterback Peyton Manning. During the 2013 season, Manning helped the Broncos score 606 points. That set an NFL record.

After the 1998 Super Bowl, more than 650,000 fans gathered in Denver to celebrate.

The Broncos made it back to the Super Bowl in 2014. But, they lost to the Seattle Seahawks 43–8.

Halftime! Stat Break

Pro Football Hall of Famers & Their Years with the Broncos

John Elway, Quarterback (1983–1998)
Floyd Little, Running Back (1967–1975)
Shannon Sharpe, Tight End (1990–1999, 2002–2003)
Gary Zimmerman, Tackle (1993–1997)

Famous Coaches

Dan Reeves (1981–1992)
Mike Shanahan (1995–2008)

Championships

SUPER BOWL APPEARANCES:
1978, 1987, 1988, 1990, 1998, 1999, 2014

SUPER BOWL WINS:
1998, 1999

Team Records

RUSHING YARDS
Career: Terrell Davis, 7,607 yards (1995–2001)
Single Season: Terrell Davis, 2,008 yards (1998)
PASSING YARDS
Career: John Elway, 51,475 yards (1983–1998)
Single Season: Peyton Manning, 5,477 yards (2013)
RECEPTIONS
Career: Rod Smith, 849 receptions (1995–2006)
Single Season: Rod Smith, 113 receptions (2001)
ALL-TIME LEADING SCORER
Jason Elam, 1,786 points, (1993–2007)

Fan Fun

STADIUM: Sports Authority Field at Mile High
LOCATION: Denver, Colorado
MASCOTS: Thunder (*left*), Miles (*above*)

Coaches' Corner

Dan Reeves became head coach of the Broncos in 1981. He coached them for 12 years. Reeves helped bring the team star players, such as John Elway. And, he led the Broncos to three Super Bowls.

Mike Shanahan took over the team in 1995. He had been an assistant coach for the Broncos for many years. He worked closely with John Elway. In 1998, Shanahan and Elway led the team to its first Super Bowl win!

Reeves was an NFL player before he became a coach. He played or coached in a record nine Super Bowls!

Before becoming head coach, Shanahan had several assistant coaching jobs with the Broncos.

Star Players

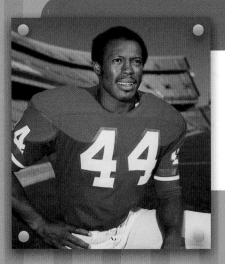

Floyd Little RUNNING BACK (1967–1975)

Floyd Little was the team's first pick in the 1967 **draft**. He was its leading rusher for his whole **career**. In 1971, he was the NFL's leading rusher. Little became a member of the Pro Football Hall of Fame in 2010.

John Elway QUARTERBACK (1983–1998)

Star quarterback John Elway led the Broncos to five Super Bowls. This included two Super Bowl wins! In 1999, Elway was named the game's MVP (Most Valuable Player). When he **retired**, Elway had 51,475 passing yards. That is more than any other Bronco. And, it is fourth in the NFL.

Terrell Davis RUNNING BACK (1995–2001)

Terrell Davis helped the team win two Super Bowls. He was named MVP of the 1998 game. The following season, he rushed for 2,008 yards. That is fifth in NFL history! That year, he was named the league's MVP.

Gary Zimmerman TACKLE (1993–1997)

Gary Zimmerman joined the Broncos in 1993. He became a leader for the team's offensive line. Zimmerman helped the Broncos win their first Super Bowl. He joined the Pro Football Hall of Fame in 2008.

Shannon Sharpe TIGHT END (1990–1999, 2002–2003)

Shannon Sharpe helped the team win two Super Bowls. When he **retired**, Sharpe had more receptions, receiving yards, and receiving touchdowns than any other tight end in the NFL. Sharpe became a member of the Pro Football Hall of Fame in 2011.

Champp Bailey CORNERBACK (2004–2013)

Champ Bailey was a strong defensive player for the Broncos. He helped the team make it to the Super Bowl in 2014. As a Bronco, Bailey played in the Pro Bowl, which is the NFL's all-star game, eight times.

Peyton Manning QUARTERBACK (2012–)

During the 2013 season, Peyton Manning threw for 5,477 yards and 55 touchdowns with the Broncos. These set NFL records! Manning was named the league's MVP. He was the first player to be named MVP five times. He led the Broncos to the 2014 Super Bowl.

Sports Authority Field at Mile High

The Broncos play home games at Sports Authority Field at Mile High. This stadium is in Denver. It holds about 76,000 people.

Sports Authority Field at Mile High opened in 2001. Before this, the Broncos played home games at Mile High Stadium. The famous Bucky Bronco statue was moved from the old stadium to the new one.

Bucky Bronco stands above a scoreboard. He can be seen from outside the stadium.

Fan Fun

Give a Salute

During the Mile High Salute, players and fans congratulate each other with a military-style salute. Terrell Davis made this practice famous in the 1990s.

Thousands of fans flock to Sports Authority Field at Mile High to see the Broncos play home games. When the team scores, some players and fans do the Mile High Salute.

The team's **mascots** are Miles and Thunder. They help fans cheer on the Broncos at home games.

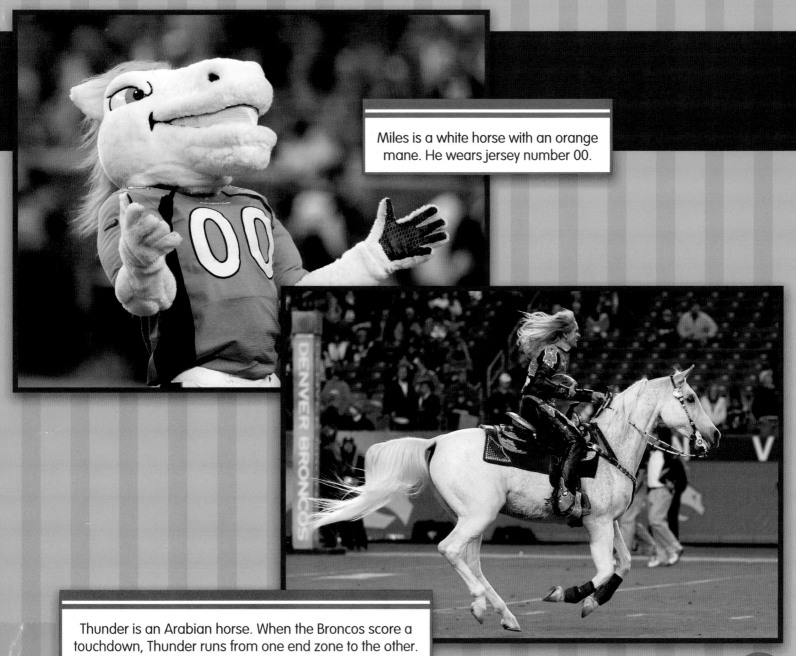

Miles is a white horse with an orange mane. He wears jersey number 00.

Thunder is an Arabian horse. When the Broncos score a touchdown, Thunder runs from one end zone to the other.

Final Call

The Broncos have a long, rich history. They have played in the Super Bowl seven times. And, they've won it twice.

Even during losing seasons, true fans have stuck by them. Many believe the Denver Broncos will remain one of the greatest teams in the NFL.

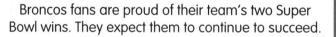

Broncos fans are proud of their team's two Super Bowl wins. They expect them to continue to succeed.

Through the Years

1960

The Denver Broncos play their first season. They are part of the AFL.

1968

The team's home stadium, Bears Stadium, is renamed Mile High Stadium.

1970

The AFL joins the NFL.

1973

The team has its first winning season.

1977

The Broncos reach the play-offs for the first time.

1978

The team plays in the Super Bowl for the first time.

1999

The team wins its second Super Bowl in a row. They beat the Atlanta Falcons 34–19.

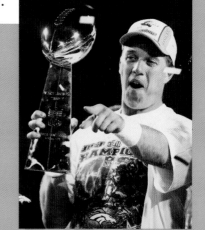

2001

Sports Authority Field at Mile High opens.

2013

Peyton Manning sets an NFL record for most single season passing yards and touchdowns.

1998

The Broncos win their first Super Bowl! They beat the Green Bay Packers 31–24.

Postgame Recap

1. Who was coach of the Broncos during their two Super Bowl wins?
    A. Dan Reeves   **B**. Terrell Davis   **C**. Mike Shanahan

2. What is the name of the stadium where the Broncos play home games?
    A. Bronco Stadium
    B. Sports Authority Field at Mile High
    C. Mile High Stadium

3. Name 2 of the 4 Broncos in the Pro Football Hall of Fame.

4. In what two ways has John Elway served the Broncos?
    A. As a player and a coach
    B. As a coach and a businessman
    C. As a player and a businessman

Glossary

career a period of time spent in a certain job.

draft a system for professional sports teams to choose new players. When a team drafts a player, they choose that player for their team.

mascot something to bring good luck and help cheer on a team.

retire to give up one's job.

Websites

To learn more about the NFL's Greatest Teams, visit **booklinks.abdopublishing.com**. These links are routinely monitored and updated to provide the most current information available.

31

Index

DATE DUE